YOSEMITE
NATIONAL PARK

Written by
VIRGINIA WOLFE
MICHAEL SCHANKERMAN

Photos by
ANDREA PISTOLESI

Contributing Photographers
Ken Glaser, Jr., Peter Lik, Philip Coblentz,
John Poimiroo, Chris Falkenstein,
Virginia Wolfe

Edited by
Ken Glaser, Jr.

BONECHI

Distribution by

SMITH NOVELTY COMPANY

460 Ninth Street
San Francisco, CA 94103
U.S.A.
Phone: 415-861-4900
Fax: 415-861-5683

YOSEMITE NATIONAL PARK

Yosemite is located near the geographical center of the Great Sierra Nevada Mountain Range in California. The park is accessible from three all-weather highways (Highway 120 from Manteca, Highway 140 from Merced and Highway 41 from Fresno), and one seasonal highway (Highway 120, accessible from US 395) from Lee Vining. Yosemite National Park is open all year round. Visitors can stay for one day or weeks exploring all the far reaches of the park. There are a wide range of accomodations from campgrounds and tent cabins to the magnificent Ahwahnee Hotel, built in 1927. Make reservations well in advance. Food, supplies and all ammenities are available in the park. For general information from the National Park Service call (209) 372-0200.

Theodore Roosevelt and John Muir
Glacier Point, Yosemite 1903

El Capitan Yosemite early 1900's

INTRODUCTION

Yosemite is one of natures finest masterpieces. The majesty and grandeur of the massive granite walls, the power of the spectacular waterfalls and the serene beauty of the valley floor, combine to create magnificent vistas in every direction. The first time visitor is in awe of the beauty and grand scale of this magical place. One feels the power of nature and the spiritual feeling that it evokes, and these feelings do not diminish as you return time after time.

Seeing Yosemite during each different season is like discovering the park for the first time. The rushing waters and lush green foliage of spring, the wild flowers and warm days of summer. The vibrant fall colors and the quiet solitude of winter with its mantel of snow all beckon for a return visit to this special place.

On the following pages our photographers have captured the essence of Yosemite. Unfortunately, a photograph can only capture the scenic vista, a place in time. They cannot pass along the emotional and spiritual feeling one derives from watching the setting sun paint the granite walls of Half Dome, while standing at the edge of Glacier Point with its 3,000 foot vertical drop. Nor can you feel the sensation of a cool spray from Vernal Fall against your face as you climb the steep Mist Trail on a warm Spring afternoon. However, these photographs will bring back memories of your visit. They will entice you to return to Yosemite National Park, where you will always continue to experience anew the beauty of one of our country's greatest natural wonders.
Enjoy!

BROAD-VALLEY STAGE

FIRST GLACIAL STAGE

MOUNTAIN-VALLEY STAGE

LAST GLACIAL STAGE

CANYON STAGE

LAKE STAGE

THE EVOLUTION OF YOSEMITE

Yosemite Valley and its surroundings were formed over hundreds of thousands of years ago as a result of uplifting in the earths crust, glaciation and erosion. Evidence of these acts of nature can be seen throughout the park in the form of glacial polish and the ancient ice scars on the giant granite domes created by ancient glaciers and the Merced River.

The first inhabitants of Yosemite Valley were native americans who enjoyed the natural beauty of this land long before Columbus discovered America. The Merced River created a natural pathway into the valley and provided a source of water, food and transportation. The Miwoks settled in the valley and lived in harmony with their surroundings until the advent of the California Gold Rush and the encroachment of civilization. Chief Tenaya and his mixed Miwok people were displaced from the area when a battalion of men led by Major James Savage entered Yosemite Valley in March of 1851. Dr. Lafayette Bunnell, the company doctor, wrote in his diary of his impressions upon seeing the magnificent monoliths and graceful waterfalls. The word traveled quickly and the first known tourists arrived in 1855.

In 1864, President Abraham Lincoln signed an Act of Congress granting Yosemite Valley and the Mariposa Grove to the state of California to be preserved for the benefit of mankind. Many people were instrumental in preserving Yosemite for future generations including, Frederick Olmstead, Galen Clark, James Hutchings, Stephen Mather and Theodore Roosevelt. John Muir is one name that is synonymous with the preservation of Yosemite. He entered the valley for the first time in 1868 at the age of 30 and revisited the valley frequently. He became increasingly alarmed at the changes he saw occuring. Finally, after years of relentless work from Muir and others, the U.S. Congress created Yosemite National Park on October 1, 1890. In 1892, Muir helped to found the Sierra Club which was dedicated to the preservation of wilderness areas. However, Muir was still not pleased having to deal with the problems relating to conflicts

between the State of California and the U.S. Army units that were stationed in the area overseeing the care of the park. Muir campaigned for total control of the park by the Federal Government. Theodore Roosevelt visited Yosemite in 1903. In 1906, he finally signed a bill to put Yosemite Valley and Mariposa Grove under the complete control of the Federal Government.

In 1907, the Yosemite Railroad began bringing visitors and by 1913 cars were permitted in the park. The final piece of the puzzle was put in place in 1916, due to the hard work of Stephen T. Mather and Horace M. Albright, when the National Park Service was created to manage all of the parks across the United States. Today, Yosemite's preservation is zealously championed by many well meaning groups and individuals. The park is still under the care and supervision of the National Park Service. Well over 3 million people visit the park every year. With this great influx, the Park Service must seek a delicate balance of useage versus preservation. A demanding job to save one of nature's treasures.

EL CAPITAN

One of the first landmarks that greets the visitor entering Yosemite Valley is the world famous El Capitan. Smooth granite rises into a single dramatic rock wall that is certainly one of the most beautiful mountain faces in the world. Incredible as it may seem, El Capitan rises to a sheer 3,000 foot ascent. Impossibly steep, even overhanging in some places, it would easily dwarf the largest of manmade structures.

The beautiful proportions of El Capitan makes it appear much smaller. When viewing El Capitan focus on the tiny trees barely visible at the summit. Those green patches which only look like bushes are actually Ponderosa and Jefferey Pines that are well over 100 feet in height.

If you spend some time viewing El Capitan you will see the sunlight play across the artfully carved rock face. Occasionally, when swirling clouds pass-by partway up the cliff, the immensity of El Capitan is more easily understood. Features will appear and disappear as the light changes through the day. Many have claimed to see the large heart carved into the west (left) face, and the darkened rock forming a map of North America on the east (right) face. The heart, the North American Wall, and the prominent central prow (called the Nose) are among some very special landmarks known to the world's best climbers. Since the 1950's, El Capitan has continued to be a mecca for climbers throughout the world. El Capitan is truly the guardian of the entrance to Yosemite Valley.

CLIMBING HISTORY

Peak bagging, one of rock climbing's earliest forms, occurred in Yosemite around the 1860's with the influx of early valley settlers. Modern day technical rock climbing traces its beginnings as far back as 1875, when George Anderson first bolted a rope to the rock curve of Half Dome's shoulder. The true technical sport of climbing took off in the 1930's, influenced by European climbers who had been challenging wilderness peaks for years. Ascents of Cathedral Spires and Royal Arches were popular during these years by many young men who later became the backbone of environmental movements. Among them were David Brower and Dick Leonard. A noteable first climber, John Salathe, arrived in the park in 1945. Salathe's pitons of hardened iron, for Yosemite's difficult rock cracks, enabled the first bold attempts and technical approaches to the sheer rock walls. Another noted climber, Warren Hading, made the epic first ascent in 1958 of El Capitan's Nose route. The widely covered and publicized event helped lend to climbing's radical reputation. Other famous names, Yvon Chouinard and Royal Robins are credited with incredible climbing firsts at Yosemite. They are also known for world famous climbing gear and outdoor adventure clothing. Yosemite had become the cutting edge of the climbing world.

Rates of climbing capability were pushed to new standards. Hardware and gear improvements were developed by the up and coming hard core climbers. New climbing aids such as springloaded camming devices and sticky soled shoes were concepts developed withinYosemite's sacred boundaries. In May of 1969, the world renowned Yosemite Mountaineering School began its reputable career in teaching this progressive sport. It was directed by Wayne Merry, who was on the first ascent of El Capitan. It was staffed by local climbers who made Yosemite their home in the effort to be in continual communion with the rock. Some of climbing's finest have guided under the School's auspices, and still do today.

Climbing continues to be progressive in Yosemite and is exemplified by a landmark ascent of El Capitan, July 1989 by two local residents. This climb was so remarkable because Mark Wellman, a ranger for the National Park Service at the time, is a paraplegic. Injured in a climbing accident several years before, his desire to climb remained strong. Partnered with Mike Corbett, already famous as Mr. El Capitan for his world record number of ascents, Mark's dream to climb El Capitan became reality. Innovative gear, herculean effort and sheer determination enabled them to accomplish the impossible. Miraculous the first time, the challenge was met once again on the face of Half Dome in September, 1991. These feats epitomize the essence of Yosemite climbing . . . bold, aggressive and creative.

Due to increased interest in climbing and the high impact on the natural resources, the National Park Service is developing a Climbing Management Plan. Climbing use and impact studies are being conducted and will eventually result in monitored and controlled access to protect Yosemite's ''vertical wilderness.''

Perhaps one of the first dramatic views many people experience is the scene on the following page. Seen from Highway 41 immediately after exiting the Wawona Tunnel. This scenic stop is known as Tunnel View, but is often mistaken for Inspiration Point, which is accessible by a 1-1/4 mile trail beginning in the upper parking area. The view from here is truly inspirational and is one of the best and most convenient stops to comprehend the layout and scope of Yosemite Valley.

On the left is El Capitan. Opposite, on the right, is Bridalveil Fall, flanked by the Leaning Tower on its right and the Cathedral Rocks rising on to its left. Behind a receding succession is Sentinel Rock, Half Dome and Cloud's Rest at the far end of the valley.

The base elevation of the U-shaped, glacially scooped valley averages about 4,000 feet above sea level. The rims rise an average of 3,000 feet almost straight up. This view deserves your attention even if you've arrived by or are exiting via another route through the park. From this vista, Yosemite's most famous photographer, Ansel Adams, captured the well-known image Clearing Winter Storm. At any given time of the day or early evening you will see professional and amateur photographers trying to create a classic image of their own.

HALF DOME

Half Dome rises majestically 4,882 feet above the valley floor at its eastern end. The most conspicuous dome, it is most frequently used as Yosemite's signature feature. During the summer months and into late fall, the summit can be reached by an 8-1/2 mile trail. The trail starts at Happy Isles and ends, after climbing a steep cable-assisted section of the dome's left sloping shoulder. The first successful climb of Half Dome was achieved by Mariposa area resident George Anderson in October of 1875. He attached a rope to the rock surface using iron eyebolts allowing easy access to the 13-acre top for other spirited adventurers to follow. After a snow avalanche tore down the rope in 1884, not much traffic went to the top. Thirty-five years later, in 1919, the Sierra Club erected the first set of steel cables. From on top, hikers can see far up Tenaya Canyon into the backcountry and many of the prominent peaks of the Tuolumne area, as well as, deep into the lush green of Yosemite Valley. Glacial action sheered away the 2,000 foot face of this solid block of granite. Left behind was an easel for nature to paint the impression of a beautiful woman with black staining lichens and algaes that grow on the surface. Derived from one of the local Indian legends this imaginative feature and the dome itself are called TIS-SA-ACK.

THREE BROTHERS

The name of this rock formation is in honor of Chief Tenaya's three sons. Ascending upwards like gables of a church, these blocks of granite owe their form to master joints, fractures in the rock that geologically criss cross the Sierras. This same triangulation of the cliffs is apparent in several other places in the valley - Glacier Point and to the right of Indian Canyon. Past and present rockslide activity in the Three Brothers area has changed the face of the middle brother and is evident by the growing talus slope below. It reminds us that we are still in an ever changing wilderness. The topmost point, aptly named Eagle Peak, tops out at 7,779 feet, that is 3,779 feet above the valley floor. It is the highest point on the north rim and is another day hike destination from a trail at the top of the Yosemite Falls.

CATHEDRAL ROCKS AND SPIRES

Forming the backdrop of Bridalveil Fall, Cathedral Rocks is remembered by old-timers as The Three Graces. Best visible from El Capitan bridge and meadow, the spires were named by early park resident James Hutchings in 1862. Another early chronicler, the Ahwahneechee Indians, had named the spires POO-SEE-NA-CHUC-KA (Mouse-proof Rocks), due to their resemblance of the log food storage caches. Both spires average 2,000 feet in height off the valley floor.

SENTINEL ROCK

Sentinel Rock is one of the more dramatic granite outcroppings looming over the valley. It's summit is 3,073 feet above the valley floor, and the rock was named for it's resemblance to a great watch-tower. It was formed by glacial action hundreds of thousands of years ago during the Ice Age. Sentinel Fall can be seen to the right of the rock as Sentinel Creek finds its way down to the Merced River on the valley floor. Behind Sentinel Fall is Sentinel Dome which is accessible only by foot. The summit of Sentinel Dome, at 8,122 feet, offers some of the finest views of the valley.

MERCED RIVER

The Merced River threads a meandering course through the seven miles of Yosemite Valley from major drainages in the surrounding high country. It races out of the valley and down a steep gorge to El Portal: it then flows 18 miles through the Merced River Canyon, meeting up with Highway 140 from Mariposa. The river's wild course ends at Bagby Dam, several miles away, in the lower foothills and contributes irrigation water to California's Central Valley agriculture. This lower section of the Merced gained wild and scenic status after grass-roots efforts evolved to save it from proposed plans to build a hydro-electric dam in the 1980's. During the summer months the river becomes a literal playground. After the spring thaw, the swollen river subsides to a lazy drift for rafters and floaters, providing one of the best ways to see Yosemite Valley. Swimming and wading are enjoyed more when the weather heats up. After a brisk refreshing dip in the clear melted snow water you can thaw out on the hot sands of the riverbank.

Although fishing has not recently been heralded in the valley, it does provide a relaxing opportunity to enjoy a pleasant day in the valley. A fishing license is required and recent regulations by the National Park Service restricts use of barbed hooks in certain areas on the river. Efforts are being made to increase native fish populations. Studies and refurbishment programs are now taking place to restore the rivers banks effected by the impact of recreational useage.

The seasonal changes are most noticeable from the banks of the Merced. During the fall and winter, receding water leaves still pools that reflect mirror images of the surrounding valley walls. Portions of the river freeze creating sheets of ice that become a canvas for the swirling water underneath. Rocks covered with a cap of pure white snow sometimes sport a collar of paper thin ice.

The various habitats inside the park provide nesting, perching and hunting sites for over 120 species of birds. Sitting quietly along the river, you may be lucky to spot the celebrated little bird, the Water Ouzel, unique for its underwater dives and forages for food. Mallard ducks nest here from spring through summer raising their ducklings along the

marshy areas of the river, later floating beside
the many rafters hoping for a handout.
Birdwatchers can usually spot the occasional
Belted Kingfisher, numerous Redwinged
Blackbirds, Flycatchers, Flickers and
Woodpeckers. One of the most common birds
is the Steller's Jay, with its bright blue body
and dark crested head. The noisy jays can be
seen throughout the park and are very popular
with the visitors. The lower Merced Gorge
provides a habitat for Golden Eagles that nest
in the more remote reaches of the canyon.
The acrobatic Peregrine Falcon can also be
seen in Yosemite Valley, and are known for
their spectacular vertical dives. Climbers on El
Capitan have compared the sound of these
vertical dives to that of a jet plane going by as
they travel over 200 m.p.h.
Yosemite is home to a variety of mammals,
many of which live on the valley floor. Among
the most commonly seen are mule deer,
raccoons, skunks, rabbits, squirrels,
chipmunks, foxes and coyotes. The American
Black Bear (usually brown in color) and the
cougar or mountain lion are living in the park
and can be dangerous, so it is very important
to remember that they should be viewed from
a distance. Also, never feed any of the animals
and give them the respect they deserve while
you visit their home.

THE CHAPEL

Over 110 years old, the quaint Yosemite Chapel was the first structure in Yosemite to be included in the National Register of Historic Places in 1973. This is also the first building seen on the right hand side of the incoming valley loop. It presents a striking contrast to what has often been referred as Nature's Cathedral. Lovely photographic opportunities abound here, especially in spring and fall as the oak trees change their color. Serving the local community and visitors from near and far, the interfaith chapel is used for church services, memorial services as well as, numerous wedding ceremonies. It has also been the place of worship for many visiting dignitaries. Church members and local community residents support and participate in overseeing the operation and continued upkeep of this small church.

THE AHWAHNEE

The grand scale of the Ahwahnee Hotel is apparent when viewing it from a distance. Inside, the grand scale continues. The dining room features a 34 foot ceiling with sugar pine support columns and floor to ceiling windows. The Great Lounge is just as spectacular. Both rooms offer great views of the surrounding natural scenery. This grand hotel gives you the feeling of stepping back in time, a time of old-fashioned elegance and simplicity. The rustic interiors, warm atmosphere and simplicity can almost make you forget that you are in the heart of one of America's most beautiful national parks. Fortunately, you are in the heart of Yosemite Valley and during the Spring, Summer and Fall it is always delightful to enjoy a light meal or drink on the rear patio. Friendly deer and other park animals can usually be spotted from this beautiful setting. The Ahwahnee was the fullfilled dream of Stephen T. Mather, the first director of the National Park System. In an innovative effort to increase funding and support for his recent charges, Mr. Mather realized that the

privileged and influential society needed to be encouraged to visit the great national treasures. In the early 1920's park visitors had to camp out or stay at minimally equipped and antiquated lodging. Mr. Mather envisioned the creation of a first-class hotel that could provide comfort within a wildrness setting. However, the development of such a hotel would require that certain details were carried forth. It had to be "special" but fit into the surrounding landscape; a new concept for the day. Such a project demanded sincere thinking and concern for the preservation of the natural surroundings. The effort began with choosing talented people suited for such a project but also familiar with Yosemite. The National Park Service and Yosemite Park and Curry Company personnel were instrumental in this search. Architect Gilbert Stanley Underwood was chosen to design the building. Curry Company's Don and Mary Tressider, family members of one of the initial hoteliers in the park, insisted on an Indian motif for the decor. Everyone involved encouraged the effort that the hotel would fit its "natural environment". Keeping with the aesthetics of The Valley, everyone agreed that the building should be entirely constructed of granite, timber and have high towering walls.

Today, even with continual renovation and maintenance the initial concept remains intact. As you walk through the lobby, the Great Lounge, and dining room, you will agree that the early men and women accomplished their grand task. In the lobby entrance there is a floor display of beautiful tile mosaics. The beams and walls throughout the Ahwahnee are bordered with designs chosen from a number of Indian baskets. Large watercolor paintings, by 1920's artist Gunnar Widforss, who captured Yosemite in a realistic watercolor style of the day, can be viewed throughout the lobby.

Other noteable features of the hotel include the mural above the fireplace in the elevator lobby or the stained glass windows in The Great Lounge. In the solarium, the immense glass windows frame the splendid landscape outside. Nearby is the Winter Club Room, which holds memories of historical winter activities in the park and across the way, the Writing Room is decorated with a mural, panelled walls and a small corner fireplace.

The Ahwahnee offers the celebrated holiday festivity, The Bracebridge Dinner, which is fashioned after Washington Irving's story of a Christmas feast, reminiscent of Medieval England. Gaily dressed players wearing 17th century costumes lead guests in carefree feasting, merriment and rejoicing of the holiday season. Every December a series of dinner plays are held. Tickets to partake in this very popular regalia are offered through a lottery system, to guarantee fair access to the limited seating. The hotel is decorated with festive ornamentations and just by walking through the lobby the excitement of the season can be shared.

Opened for business since July of 1927, the Ahwahnee Hotel has enjoyed a colorful history. Serving the well-to-do of the day along with many famous actors, politicians, wealthy socialites and royalty. One of the more recent famous visits was, the March 1983 visit of Her Majesty, Queen Elizabeth II, and His Royal Highness, Prince Philip, Duke of Edinburgh. Today, the Ahwahnee continues to entertain the world's elite, but remains accessible to all visitors whether they be a hiker, camper or tourist simply eager to catch a glimpse of a bygone era and elegance.

THE FALLS OF YOSEMITE

Quite possibly the most spectacular display of water in the valley is Yosemite Falls which is over 2,400 feet in height. It also has the distinction of being the first landmark in Yosemite Valley that was sketched and published by the artist Thomas Ayres. Beside it sits another unique feature, The Lost Arrow, which rises about 1,500 feet. Its name comes from one of the local Indian legends. Mesmerising for early season travelers who catch the falls in full force, many late summer and autumn visitors are disappointed when they see a barren, dry rock face. Yosemite's waterfalls are dependant on the winter snowpack and a rapid melt or low water content in the snow determines how long the water flows. Sometimes prolonged by heavy summer thunderstorms, the falls capacity visibly swells to torrential proportions.

The trail to the top of Upper Yosemite Falls starts approximately one-half mile west of the Lower Fall parking lot. A strenuous 2,000 foot climb, hikers are advised to carry water, wear good hiking shoes and allow a full day to rest along the way and enjoy the birds-eye views of Half Dome and Yosemite Valley.

VERNAL FALL

Yosemite is world famous for its hiking trails and one of the most beautiful and most popular is the trail to Vernal and Nevada Falls. You embark at Happy Isles, and the vertical climb begins. The sounds of the crashing water add to the drama of the spectacular scenery. The first view of Vernal Fall is from a bridge far below. Soon to come is the famous Mist Trail, a steep climb up granite blocks ever so close to the thundering waters. During the peak flow in the spring and early summer the mist can soak you to the bone. Once at the top of Vernal Fall you can relax by the Emerald Pool surrounded by slick granite, polished by the water and ice of yesteryear. After a short rest you can continue on to Nevada Fall and equally beautiful scenery. This gorgeous cascade leaps from a narrow spout and tumbles down a very impressive 594 foot drop. Halfway down the drop, the rushing water fans out into a graceful apron. This view is very rewarding to the intrepid hiker, but remember that this view can also be enjoyed from a distance by driving to Glacier Point. This is one of Yosemite's great gifts that should not be missed.

Yosemite's other falls that can be easily
viewed from the valley floor are Bridalveil Fall
and Ribbon Fall. Bridalveil Fall drops 620 feet
to the left of the Leaning Tower. It runs all
year but the flow is very light in the late
summer. Ribbon Fall to the left of El Capitan is
the highest free leaping fall in the valley at
1,612 feet. The flow from Ribbon Fall is very
short lived and is usually dry by July or
August.

GLACIER POINT

The fantastic view from Glacier Point gives the visitor a chance to finally get a clear perspective of the layout of Yosemite National Park. Directly below, overlooking a sheer 3,000 foot drop is the Curry Village complex. Across the Valley stands the grand Ahwhanee Hotel, from this dizzying height, looking like a toy castle made of pebbles. The expansive valley meadows look like tiny patches of green and brown. Tall pine trees seem like blades of grass. Even more amazing is the sweep of mountains bordering the parkland.
Breathtaking panoramas of the High Sierra crest encircle the visitor. Formations that may look like nothing more than points of rock are enormous jagged mountain summits that can only be approached by intrepid backpackers and mountaineers. On a clear day, summits can be seen that rise at least 50 miles from Glacier Point. Between Glacier Point and these

distant summits is a vast wonderland of wrinkled and carved granite that looks like waves on a storm-tossed sea frozen in time. Blanketing glaciers carved this granite wilderness into the wonderful shapes we see today. One can only imagine what fantastic changes the next ice age may bring. Streams running through the valleys continue to steepen and narrow the gorges even as we watch. These streams can be seen tumbling into Yosemite Valley forming a collection of the most beautiful waterfalls in the world.
Certainly the most dramatic landmark is Half Dome. This signature piece of sculpted granite divides the Merced River drainage from the tributary drainage of Tenaya Creek. Behind Half Dome rises the aptly named Clouds Rest, forming the largest single unbroken granite wall in the world.
Standing on Glacier Point and looking directly

east, the visitor is impressed by a pair of enormous distant waterfalls. The uppermost fall is Nevada Fall. The Merced River drops 594 feet in a graceful sweep down the angled rock face. A few hundred yards downstream Vernal Fall forms a dramatic, beautifully proportioned sheer drop of another 317 feet.

A little northward, to the left of Half Dome, an obvious but inaccessible glacial valley is named in honor of Chief Tenaya. A long graceful cascade of water at the head of Tenaya Canyon is called Pywiack Cascade. To the left of this canyon, almost directly north of Glacier Point, are the beautifully rounded Basket and North Domes. Beneath North Dome, forming the wall behind the Ahwahnee Hotel, is the unique formation called the Royal Arches. West of the Royal Arches, Yosemite Point, Lost Arrow and the Yosemite Falls complete the most prominent views.

Glacier Point was the site of one of the first inns that welcomed visitors to Yosemite. James McCauley and his wife ran the Glacier Point Mountain House from 1872 through 1897. Mr. McCauley was the creator of the famous Firefall, which became a tradition in Yosemite for years. After nightfall in the valley, burning embers would be pushed over the steep granite wall of Glacier Point and free-fall over 1,000 feet to a ledge below. This spectacular event was visible from many areas in the valley, but the most popular spot to view this event was at Camp Curry. The Firefall stopped for a few years in the late 1800's, but was started again at the turn-of-the-century by David Curry. The Curry family became the major innkeepers at Yosemite and continued the Firefall nightly during the summer months until 1968. The Glacier Point Hotel, a 90 room lodge, was built in 1917. The views were spectacular but the hotel was not very successful due to the fact that most visitors wanted to stay in the valley. Both the Inn and the hotel were destroyed by fire in 1969.

The seasonal changes in Yosemite are visible in the foliage colors that dress the trees, shrubs and grasses. Because of the altitude spread within the park, seasons strike the landscape at different times, usually beginning at the lower elevations and travelling upwards as the seasons progress.

During the spring, after a long sleepy winter, light green leaf buds begin to tip the various deciduous trees. The broadleaf maples, willows and California Black Oaks begin to redress their naked limbs with delicate tiny leaves of varying shades of new green. One of the most beautiful and dramatic trees to bloom in the spring is the Pacific Dogwood, whose large white flowering bracts dress the forest in delicate lace patterns. The dogwood, of all the indigenous trees, seems to be the most joyous to celebrate the return of the sun's warmth. Their floral fested limbs retain their decor long into June. Meadows that have been asleep under a blanket of snow begin pushing up new shoots of milkweed, green coils of bracken ferns and Indian hemp and sedges.

Summertime stabilizes in Yosemite by the consistent green that paints all the trees in the park. The deep green of the Ponderosa pines is contrasted by lighter shades created by.the

oaks and maples. The meadows go through various stages of lush green to a joyful array of flowers. Various species decorate meadows to make them appear as an artist's palette of joyful colors. Bright pink Shooting Stars, white puffy Bistorts, Blue Lupine, yellow faces of Monkey Flowers and the brilliant red of Paintbrush are just a few of the flowers that live in the meadows.

Mid to late September the first hints of autumn become visible. Dogwoods exhibit their clusters of red-orange berries. Even though the weather stays warm, the foliage starts to turn the buff and tan colors that signify summer is now dwindling. The grasses in the meadows turn brown and start to dry out. Stalks of milkweed and Indian hemp turn red, their leaves yellow. Bracken ferns turn color and look like large leaves covering the forest floor. Occasional patches of dark red peak out from green dogwood trees, hinting at the vibrant display soon due. Yosemite is fortunate to have a wide selection of deciduous trees and annual shrubs and grasses that turn color. Aspens, broadleaf maples and oaks turn the full scale of yellows, ochres and oranges. Contrasting with the bright red of the dogwood, the colors illicit a joyous response from the beholder. One cannot resist the impulse to revel in these luxurious colors.

All too soon, this special time of year gives
way to storms that knock the leaves off the
limbs, battens down the stalks of dry grass and
weeds and prepares the land for winter. While
much of the foliage in Yosemite sleeps during
the winter months, the pine and fir trees
continue to be revealed. Dark, overcast days
are brightened by images of snowcapped
peaks. The whiteness defines the shapes and
outlines of the various conifers emphasizing
their shredded red bark, blue green foliage of
sequoias and yellow green of cedars. The
large gangly limbs of the Sugar pines stand out
against the patterned backdrop of Ponderosa
pines. The yellow green of the Fruticose lichen
that grows on the trees becomes a vibrant
display.

Yosemite is a magical place to watch and
enjoy the seasons change as reflected in its
diverse foliage.

WAWONA HOTEL

Nestled six miles east of the south entrance of the park on Highway 41, the historic Wawona Hotel sits on a grassy knoll above a well-kept 18-hole golf course. The hotel, recognized as a National Historic Landmark, offers comfortable period decorated lodgings and pleasant meals in its old fashioned dining room. Wawona is often referred to by the local residents as "Yosemite's Sleepy Hollow." The hotel definitely holds that atmosphere to a time when life was slower paced and unhurried. You may sit on the wide porch sipping a cool, refreshing drink and watch bathers enjoying the small pool, water trickling down the rock fountain, or enjoy the lovely restored Hill House, once used by artist Thomas Hill as a studio.
The hotel's history is truly turn-of-the-century.

The area was initially settled by Galen Clark, Yosemite's first guardian. Clark's Station, as it was known, was later to become a rest stop on the long and dusty stagecoach road that led into the Yosemite Valley from the central valley. The dwellings and land were bought in 1874 by the enterprising Washburn Brothers, who added new buildings and upgraded the services to accommodate the ever increasing visitation to Yosemite. By the 1930's, the Park Service wanted to acquire this busy access into the National Park and in 1933 bought the land and buildings. The operation and maintenance of the hotel service went to the established Yosemite Park and Curry Company. Today, the historic atmosphere and genial hospitality are still available at Wawona.

WAWONA PIONEER MUSEUM

Neatly tucked away on the bank of the South Fork of the Merced River in Wawona, the Yosemite Pioneer History Center offers an authentic view of Yosemite's pioneer past. Included here are restored cabins, horse drawn vehicles, a covered bridge and other buildings that played an important roll in the history and development of Yosemite's yesteryear. During summer months, "living history" players dress and act the part of many of the early Yosemite residents. You can hitch a ride on an authentic horse drawn stagecoach for a ride up to the hotel and enjoy the relaxed atmosphere. Close by are a general store and gift shop that offer welcome mementos of your trip to Yosemite.

MARIPOSA GROVE

A pleasant and rewarding stop awaits you at the Mariposa Grove of Big Trees on Highway 41, just south of the entrance station. As you stroll or take a guided tram tour under the trees, you are humbled by their immense size. This grove, named by Galen Clark, was set aside in 1864, along with Yosemite Valley, as the first protected areas in the United States. It is one of three groves within the boundary of

Yosemite National Park.

Interpretive signs are scattered around the points of interest along the road. A representation of Galen Clark's cabin sits picturesquely in a clearing below some of the massive conifers and houses the local museum where during summer and fall publications are offered for sale. Ranger led walks and signs declare the important roll that fire performs in the maturation and promotion of the sequoias. Studies have shown the trees regenerate in the enriched soil left after a fire and are strengthened by the sun allowed in by the clearing of brush on the forest floor. The root systems of these mammoths are very shallow and credited for the toppling that has occurred to several of the larger trees. Due to the high tannin in the heartwood, they are extremely slow to decay. This inside wood is only vulnerable to fire and is normally protected by the fire-retardant, shreddy, outer bark. This is probably why these trees have reached an estimated lifespan of up to 3,000 years and are considered to be the largest living thing on earth.

HIGH COUNTRY

Most visitors are surprised to learn that
Yosemite Valley is just a small part of
Yosemite National Park. A vast wilderness,
including the entire watershed of the mighty
Merced and Tuolumne Rivers, sprawls over
1,170 square miles. Rugged mountain peaks,
rising over 13,000 feet, ring this wonderland.
The high mountain slopes collect heavy winter
snows. In summer, this snowpack steadily
melts in the glaring high altitude sunlight,
forming a myriad of crystal clear brooks and
streams. These streams collect into alpine
lakes that lie scattered like jewels at the head
of tremendous granite gorges. A few fortunate
backpackers and mountaineers wander
through this region, savoring some of the most
beautiful scenery in the world. These
spectacular areas are only visited by a small
percentage of the people that come to the
park. The High Country is a sort of holy land
for the many wilderness enthusiasts and we
are all enriched by the preservation of this
region.

TIOGA PASS

Bisecting Yosemite from the east side of the Sierra, directly up the Lee Vining Canyon is Yosemite's east entrance, the Tioga Pass at an elevation of 9,941 feet. Snow pack determines the opening and closing of this seasonal road, but it is usually open between mid June and late October. This pass was used by Native Americans on both sides of the Sierra, possibly as a trade route, in prerecorded times. It became a popular access route for the exploration of miners seeking silver and gold during the late 1800's. Beginning as a foot trail, it was later widened to accommodate mining wagons, and eventually acquired in the early 1900's by Park Service officials to gain the easy access and thoroughfare through Yosemite National Park. Guarded by Mt. Dana on one side, entry into the park from this entrance gives the park visitor a panoramic view of the famous Yosemite with lesser known, but none-the-less dynamic landscape.

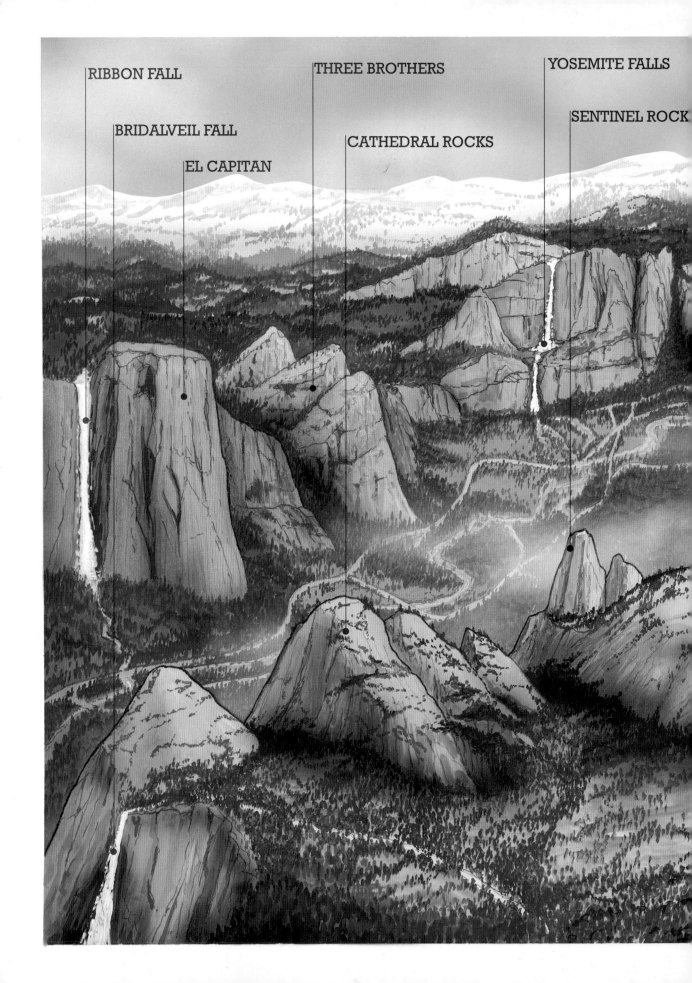

RIBBON FALL

BRIDALVEIL FALL

EL CAPITAN

THREE BROTHERS

CATHEDRAL ROCKS

YOSEMITE FALLS

SENTINEL ROCK

YOSEMITE VILLAGE

ROYAL ARCHES

GLACIER POINT

MIRROR LAKE

HALF DOME

VERNAL FALL

NEVADA FALL

Benini '93

INDEX

© Copyright 1994 by CASA EDITRICE BONECHI
Via Cairoli 18/b - 50131 FIRENZE - ITALY
Telex 571323 CEB - Fax 55/5000766

*All rights reserved. No part of this publication
may be reproduced without the
written permission of the Publisher.*

The photos by *Andrea Pistolesi*
are the property of Casa Editrice Bonechi
Map of Yosemite by *Stefano Benini*
Printed in Italy by Centro Stampa Editoriale Bonechi

ISBN 88-7009-972-5

PHOTO CREDITS

All photos by ANDREA PISTOLESI except the following:
Philip Coblentz: pages 18-19, page 29 (top), page 30
(bottom), page 52 (top right), page 59 (center), page 60
(top), page 61 (top)
Chris Falkenstein: page 14
Ken Glaser, Jr.: page 29 (bottom), page 33, page 35
(bottom), page 45 (bottom), page 51 (top), page 52 (top left),
page 53 (top), page 59 (bottom)
Peter Lik: page 1, pages 10-11, page 17 (left)
National Park Service (Yosemite Collection): page 6
John Poimiroo: page 32
Virginia Wolfe: page 24
Yosemite Park and Curry Company (Communication
Department): page 3, page 7 (bottom),
page 9 (top), page 47, page 51, page 56